WINGS OVER DENALI

D0879344

WINGS OVER

Denali from east of Ruth Gorge, July 1987. Lowell Thomas Jr.

DENALI

A Photographic History of Aviation in Denali National Park

BRUCE McALLISTER

FOREWORD BY
LOWELL THOMAS JR.

ROUNDUP PRESS

BOULDER, COLORADO, U.S.A.

In memory of the climbers and pilots who have lost their lives on Denali

© 2004 by Bruce McAllister

All rights reserved. No part of this book may be
reproduced, stored in a retrieval system or
transmitted in any form or by any means
without written permission of the publisher.

Roundup Press, P.O. Box 109, Boulder, CO 80306-0109

Library of Congress Control Number 2003098412
ISBN 0-9638817-6-0

BOOK DESIGN
Paulette Livers, Livers Lambert Design, Boulder, CO

PHOTOGRAPHY EDITOR
Bruce McAllister

PHOTO CREDITS
Front Cover: Denali from the east. ©Bruce McAllister
Back Cover: Unloading skiers from
a Cessna 185 aircraft at west fork of Ruth Gorge near
Denali. Dog in the foreground is "Piney." ©Dick Stone

SPECIAL THANKS TO
Lowell Thomas Jr. and Kitty Banner Seemann

ACKNOWLEDGMENTS
Randy & Marion Acord
Bill Bacon III
Ann Kain, Denali National Park and Preserve
Scott Darsey
Annie Duquette
Mike Fisher
Major Michael L. Haller, Alaska National Guard
Don Lee
Jim Okonek
Colonel Ron Parkhouse, Alaska National Guard
Roger Robinson, Denali National Park and Preserve
Holly Sheldon
Dick Stone
Francis "Twigg" Twigg
Bradford Washburn

DISCLAIMER
*The author has attempted to give accurate aeronautical information. He cannot
be held responsible for the accuracy of this information and it is not to be used for
navigational purposes.*

ALSO AVAILABLE FROM ROUNDUP PRESS:

Wings Across America ISBN 0-9638817-9-5 $39.95 (Add $5.00 for P&H)

Wings Above the Arctic ISBN 0-9638817-8-7 $39.95 (Add $5.00 for P&H)

Wings Over the Alaska Highway ISBN 0-9638817-7-9 $34.95 (Add $5.00 for P&H)

Printed and bound in China by C&C Offset Printing Co.

CONTENTS

FOREWORD

Flying Mount Denali (formerly called Mount McKinley) has been one of the most rewarding experiences of my life. My first encounter with North America's tallest mountain came while I was producing a television film about our new state, Alaska, during the summer of 1958. As I looked at the four-mile-high mass of sparkling snow and ice from my Cessna 180, it beckoned me like the flame of a candle beckons a moth. But it was twenty years before I began to fly Denali as a full-time commercial pilot and owner of Talkeetna Air Taxi and Thomas Air. Then, for the next fifteen years I flew mountain climbers on and off the mountain's glaciers, took visitors "flight-seeing," and made frequent ski landings in the Don Sheldon amphitheater.

What was so rewarding about that time? Not the money—I was lucky to break even most years. No, it was the way of life: flying a small plane with

Lowell Thomas Jr. on Denali. Lowell Thomas Jr.

wheel/skis among the most majestic and challenging mountains on our planet with ever-changing conditions in the weather and the glaciers' surface.

The challenge was to cope with Denali's fickle nature—to read its moods and to know when a mission might or might not succeed. Along with poor visibility, when clouds, snow, and fog hung about, the greatest threat I faced was from downdrafts. Winds blowing over the summit and along its many ridges produce invisible updrafts and downdrafts strong enough to toss a plane thousands of feet up or down—down being the more perilous. Only experience taught me how to read nature's warning signs, such as snow blowing off ridges, cloud formations and their movement, and the direction of upper winds. I'll never forget one experience. I was on a high-altitude search for a missing solo climber, and I found myself cruising at 20,000 feet along the north side of Denali. The air was smooth and cold; the temperature was minus twenty degrees. There were no snow streamers off the summit, no cloud cap, and no sign of wind. But just as I reached the mountain's east side, the bottom fell out. The plane and I went into a freefall, still flying but in a plunging air mass that in less than thirty seconds delivered us out over the northwest fork of Ruth Glacier at 14,000 feet—an incredible rate of descent of at least 12,000 feet per minute! Plane and I had experienced an aerial Niagara Falls. Fortunately, our eastward momentum carried us beyond the rock and ice cliffs of Denali's east face.

Dangerous living, for sure! During my years of flying that mountain, there have been at least half-a-dozen crashes, most of them fatal. I would attribute nearly all the crashes to unexpected downdrafts in places where there was not enough altitude to escape. But the very danger of mountain flying is a large part of its appeal. It's the challenge along with the fun and adventure—and the wild scenic beauty.

All of this comes across to the reader of this stunningly beautiful book, *Wings Over Denali*.

—*Lowell Thomas Jr.*
Lt. Governor, Alaska, 1974–1978
Owner/Operator Talkeetna Air Taxi, 1980–1988

Bob Reeve used a Fairchild 51 aircraft on skis to deliver CAT parts on Columbia Glacier, one mile from the Rough & Tough Mine. Reeve was probably the first Alaska bush pilot to do extensive glacier landings, and his son-in-law, Don Sheldon, went on to gain fame for landings on Denali's glaciers. Date unknown.
Russ Dow—Museum of Alaska Transportation & Industry, Wasilla

Opposite: ©NGS Image Collection

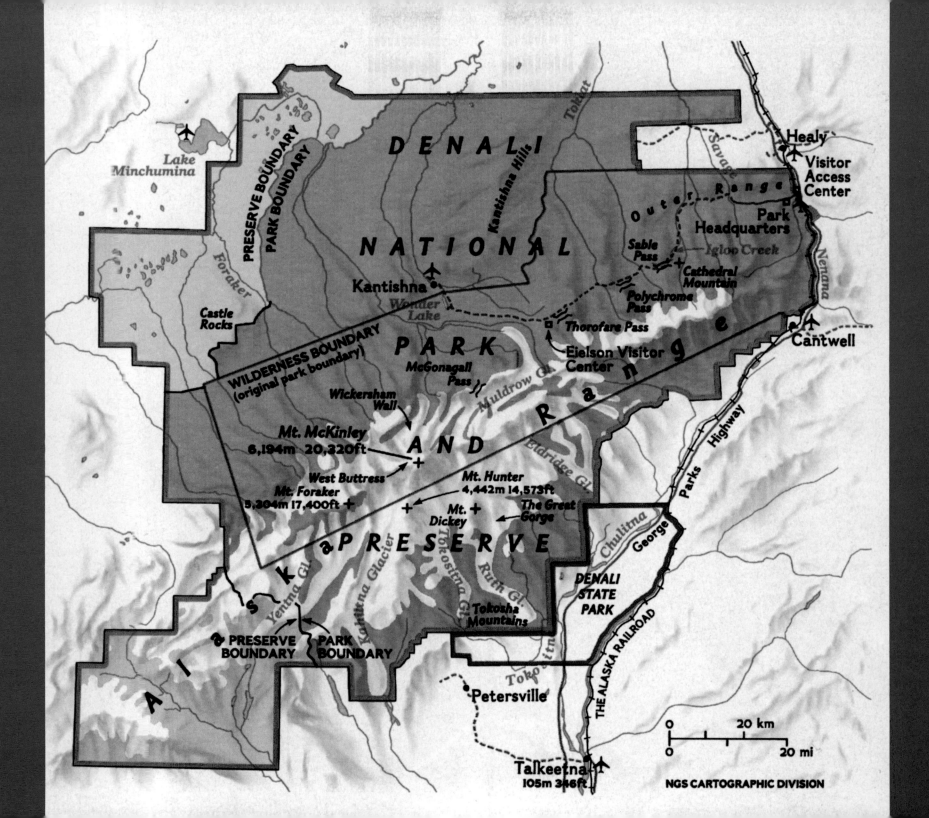

DENALI NATIONAL PARK AND PRESERVE

Lake Minchumina

PRESERVE BOUNDARY

PARK BOUNDARY

Kantishna Hills

Tokat

Healy

Visitor Access Center

Outer Range

Park Headquarters

Igloo Creek

Sable Pass

Kantishna

Cathedral Mountain

Wonder Lake

Polychrome Pass

Castle Rocks

Foraker

WILDERNESS BOUNDARY
(original park boundary)

Thorofare Pass

Eielson Visitor Center

McGonagall Pass

Muldrow Gl.

Cantwell

Nenana

Wickersham Wall

Mt. McKinley
6,194m 20,320ft

West Buttress

Eldridge Gl.

Parks Highway

Mt. Foraker
5,304m 17,400ft

Mt. Hunter
4,442m 14,573ft

The Great Gorge

Mt. Dickey

Chulitna

George

DENALI STATE PARK

Yentna Gl.

Kahiltna Glacier

Tokositna Gl.

Ruth Gl.

PRESERVE BOUNDARY

PARK BOUNDARY

Tokosha Mountains

THE ALASKA RAILROAD

Tokositna

Petersville

20 km

20 mi

Talkeetna
105m 346ft

NGS CARTOGRAPHIC DIVISION

According to Bradford Washburn, the great climber and aerial photographer, who probably knows Denali better than any other person, Dr. Frederick A. Cook described the mountain best. In a 1903 magazine article, he wrote: "The area of this mountain is far inland, in the heart of a most difficult and trackless country, making the transportation of men and supplies a very arduous task. The thick underbrush, the endless marshes, and the myriads of vicious mosquitoes bring to the traveler the troubles of the tropics … [and] the discomforts of the arctic explorer; the very difficult slopes, combined with high altitude effects, add the troubles of the worst Alpine climbs."[4] The glacier pilots who fly the Denali area also must deal with hidden crevasses at landing spots, vicious winds, whiteouts, and fast-moving fronts.

Sheldon to the present, pilots flying Denali have displayed guts, skill, and experience, and have had more than a little luck. Most landings in the park are on glacier fields at high altitudes. For this very reason, Don Sheldon did not paint his aircraft. The slight payload gain from eliminating the weight of a paint job enabled him to get better high-altitude performance from his aircraft. No two flights into the park are the same—pilots learn the country fast or don't come back.

Alaska pilots are different from most lower-48 pilots. Some even think that an unplanned off-field landing is a prerequisite for joining the fraternity of

---

Above: This old billboard promotes the benefits of flying in the Denali area in the 1930s.© Bruce McAllister

Opposite: Bob Reeve with his Fairchild 71 aircraft after landing on Brevier Glacier in the Chugach Range, at an elevation of 6,000 feet, near the Big 4 Mine. Note three flags at left, which marked his uphill landing path. Date unknown.
Russ Dow—Museum of Alaska Transportation & Industry, Wasilla

Guide Ray Genet (left) and Dave Thomas on the summit of Mount Denali in May 1979. Genet perished on Mount Everest later that year, but during his career he climbed Denali twenty-four times.
Lowell Thomas Jr.

Opposite: Lowell Thomas Jr. (left) and three Russian climbers at Kahiltna base camp in May 1986.
Lowell Thomas Jr.

Bud Helmericks, October 2001. ©Bruce McAllister

pilots. Insurance is so expensive that some pilots do not carry hull insurance—especially after they have left their aircraft on a sandbar. "All [Alaska] pilots know that if they stay with the game long enough in this country they will eventually spin in. One's luck can't be with him all the time. There are exploits in flying in Alaska that would make all other flying stories any place look dull by comparison."[5] This observation might sound a bit extreme, but that's how Constance Helmericks saw Alaska aviation in 1944 when she wrote *We Live in Alaska*. Her husband, Bud Helmericks, later became one of Alaska's most famous bush pilots and proved that resourceful pilots could do better "than spin in." As of 2003, they both were retired and living in Fairbanks.

A Helio Courier, piloted by Lowell Thomas Jr., flying over Denali's West Buttress.
©Roger Robinson

A Star Airways Ford Trimotor aircraft takes on passengers and freight at McGrath, Alaska. The aircraft was probably on a run between Anchorage and McGrath in the late 1930s. Anchorage Museum of History & Art

Opposite: In the early 1930s, these three Stinson SM-1DB Detroiter aircraft on skis were often used to carry furs in the winter from places like the Arctic and interior Alaska to Anchorage. Each aircraft had a range of 750 miles. Anchorage Museum of History & Art

CHAPTER 1
Chronology of Firsts in Aviation History on Denali

This chronology lists the progression of altitude records established by different types of aircraft that have landed on Denali. It does not include all landings, but does include notable firsts. All elevations are in feet above sea level. *(National Park Ranger Roger Robinson supplied the original list.)*

Fixed-Wing Aircraft Firsts

August 13, 1930: 24,000 feet, over Denali summit. Pilot Matt Nieminen and mechanic Cecil Higgins flew a Fairchild 71 aircraft, NC9153, to 24,000 feet over Denali to shoot aerial still photographs and motion pictures.

August 29, 1931: 20,320 feet, Denali summit. Pilot Joe Crosson flew by the summit without oxygen in a Fairchild 71 aircraft to determine the correct elevation of Denali. The aircraft had four altimeters on board to make the historic calculation.

April 25, 1932: 6,100 feet, Muldrow Glacier. Pilot Joe Crosson, in a Fairchild 71, NC9745, landed at 6,100 feet (in support of the Cosmic Ray Expedition).

May 16, 1932: 6,100 feet, Muldrow Glacier. Pilot Jerry Jones, in a Stearman C2-B 5415, performed an air medevac operation at 6,100 feet. Jones flew in from a muddy, grass landing strip outside Fairbanks; the

---

Buddy Woods landing a helicopter near Denali's summit in 1976 for a spectacular rescue. Ray Genet

airstrip had been wet down by the fire department so that he could take off with skis. He rescued Edward Beckwith of the Cosmic Ray Expedition.

June 25, 1951: 10,000 feet, Kahiltna Pass. Pilot Terris Moore landed at 10,000 feet in a Super Cub 150, N1088A. He also made several landings at lower elevations in support of the first ascent of the West Buttress.

Late June 1959: 16,200 feet, Mount Sanford summit. Pilot Terris Moore landed his modified Piper Super Cub, N2584P, (with a newly released Lycoming 160-horsepower engine, modified wings, and prop) on the summit. Two Army Piasecki H-21 helicopters followed him to the summit, were able to land, and then take off. Although Mount Sanford is not in the Denali area, this was a very significant glacier landing in Alaska aviation history. His aircraft held the world's altitude record for landing and taking off until 1960; in that year, a Pilatus Porter landed at around 17,000 feet in the Himalayas.

May 20–26, 1960: 14,200 feet, West Buttress. Three pilots made multiple landings at 14,200 feet: Don Sheldon in a Super Cub 150 (eight landings), George Kitchen in a Super Cub 150 (two landings), and Jack Wilson in a Super Cub 150 (one landing). These landings were in support of the John Day rescue.

June 19, 1976: 14,200 feet, West Buttress. Pilot Doug Geeting, with Ranger Nick Hartzel, landed a Cessna 185 at 14,200 feet to check its performance.

June 2, 1977: 14,200 feet, West Buttress. Pilot Jim Sharp landed a Cessna 185 at 14,200 feet to rescue an injured climber (Ratliff).

June 10, 1983: 14,200 feet, West Buttress. Pilot Lowell Thomas Jr., with Ranger Roger Robinson, landed his turbocharged Helio Courier in support of the medical research camp. Over the next five years, Thomas made thirteen landings to supply the camp and assist in rescues.

One of the hang gliders that was successfully flown off the top of Denali on June 4, 1976, is on display at the Museum of Transportation & Industry in Wasilla, Alaska. ©Bruce McAllister

Helicopter Firsts

September 1949: 5,700 feet, Muldrow Glacier. Lieutenant Colonel Bill Weed and co-pilot Slim Linebaugh made several landings in this area in a U.S. Air Force Sikorsky H-5-G, in support of the Office of Naval Research, Bradford Washburn, and Jim Gale.

May 31, 1954: 5,500 feet, Muldrow Glacier (opposite McGonagall Pass). Captain Searle of the U.S. Army's 74th Rescue Squadron, in an unknown type of helicopter, rescued George Argus of the Thayer Traverse Expedition. (Argus sustained injuries to a hip, knees, chest, and head.)

May 20, 1960: 17,200 feet, West Buttress. Pilot Link Luckett made four landings in a Hiller 12-E to rescue John Day (fall injuries) and Pete Schoening (frostbite).

June 28, 1970: 15,000 feet, Harper Basin. An unknown U.S. Air Force pilot, in a Bell UH-1 Huey, rescued Tom Kensler (cerebral edema).

June 4, 1972: 17,200 feet, West Buttress. Pilot Gene Lloyd, in an Aérospatiale Alouette III, rescued Dick Witte (broken leg).

April 7, 1976: 17,200 feet, West Buttress. An unknown pilot, in an Army Boeing Vertol CH-47-C Chinook (High-Altitude Rescue Team, HART), rescued Hanspeter Trachsel (broken ankle).

May 18, 1976: 15,000 feet, Harper Basin. An unknown pilot, in a Bell 205, rescued Charles Gasser (pulmonary edema).

June 3, 1976: 20,300 feet, a few yards southeast of the summit. Pilot Buddy Woods, in a Hiller 12-J-3, rescued Jennifer Williams and Paula Kregel (injuries from a fall). For this rescue Woods landed two times at 16,000 feet, two times at 19,600 feet, one time at 20,100 feet (supply drop-off), one time at summit (Ray Genet drop-off), four times at 18,700 feet (northeast South Peak). Genet assisted a climber at 19,600 feet and a second one at 18,700 feet. Another rescuer, Greg Ballog, was dropped off and picked up at 18,700 feet.

June 11, 1978: 18,200 feet, Denali Pass. An unknown pilot, in a Boeing Vertol CH-47-C Chinook (HART), rescued Bruce Hickson (cerebral edema), Tom Crouch (acute mountain sickness), and George Gonzales (unknown ailment).

July 28, 1979: 16,200 feet, South Face. An unknown pilot, in a Boeing Vertol CH-47-C Chinook (HART), hoisted Mitsuyasu Hamatani (unknown ailment) off the South Face.

June 16, 1980: 16,100 feet, Harper Basin. An unknown pilot, with Ranger Bob Gerhard, in a Bell 206, rescued Jan Mikeska (unknown ailment).

May 6, 1982: 16,900 feet, West Rib. Pilot Chris Soloy, with Ranger Scott Gill, in a Hiller-Turbine 1100, rescued Alan Pohl (pulmonary edema).

Fellow pilot Dick Stone took this dramatic photograph of Lowell Thomas Jr. taking off from Denali at an elevation of 14,200 feet. The turbocharged Helio Courier he was flying was known for its short takeoff and landing capability. Date unknown. ©Dick Stone

July 27, 1983: 17,200 feet, West Buttress. Pilot Ron Smith, with Ranger Scott Gill, in a Bell 212, rescued Liao Kun-Shan (pulmonary edema).

May 27, 1988: 18,200 feet, Cassin Ridge. Chief Warrant Officer Four Myron Babcock, with Randy Mullen, in a Boeing Vertol CH-47-C Chinook (HART), coordinated an 80-foot hoist off Cassin Ridge, rescuing Sung Hyun Baek (with altitude illness and frostbite). On June 3, 1988, at the same location two more hoists were performed, one by Babcock and the other by Chip Brown.

May 24, 1991: 14,200 feet, West Buttress. Lieutenant Colonel Terry Graybeal and Lieutenant Colonel Ron Parkhouse, in an Alaska Air National Guard Sikorsky MH-60 Pavehawk, rescued Kim Hongbim (frostbite and pulmonary edema). The flight crew on this mission all received Airmen's Medals.

July 5, 1991: 19,600 feet, a football-sized field near the summit. Pilot Jim Hood, in an Aérospatiale SA-315B Lama (NPS), made four landings in the rescue of Krzysztof Wiecha. Rangers Daryl Miller and Jim Phillips assisted in this rescue effort.

May 18, 1992: 17,700 feet, Cassin Ridge. Pilot Bill Ramsey, with Ranger Jim Phillips, in an Aérospatiale SA-315B Lama (NPS), made three difficult landings to rescue three Koreans.

June 8, 1993: 20,320 feet, Summit. Pilot Bill Ramsey, in an Aérospatiale SA-315B Lama (NPS), short-hauled Ranger Daryl Miller from the 14,200-foot camp to the summit and back.

June 9, 1995: 19,600 feet, on slopes of Denali. Chief Warrant Officer Four Bill Barker, in a Boeing Vertol CH47-D Chinook (HART), landed twice at the spot where volunteers Alex Lowe, Conrad Anker, Scott Backes, and Marc Twight provided assistance in the rescue of two Spanish climbers (frostbite and altitude illness).

June 17, 1995: 20,320 feet, Summit. Pilot Doug Drury, in an Aérospatiale SA-315B Lama (NPS), landed on the summit.

June 22, 1998: 19,000 feet, West Rib short haul. Pilot Jim Hood, in an Aérospatiale SA-315B Lama (NPS), rescued two British climbers in one short haul to 14,200 feet.

Improvements in Denali Helicopter Operations

The army activated the High-Altitude Rescue Team (HART) in 1973 after a military aircraft crashed at 14,000 feet on Mount Sanford in the Wrangell Mountains. The original Boeing Vertol CH-47-A Chinook was used for this rescue. Beginning in 1982, HART has been instrumental in depositing and extracting personnel and equipment at a camp at 14,200 feet on the popular West Buttress route. Dr. Peter Hackett led this research until 1990. In 1991, the National Park Service installed a smaller version of the camp with the continued support of HART. HART acts as a back-up to the NPS Aérospatiale SA-315B Lama helicopter and responds to all high-mountain rescues throughout the state.

Also in 1991, the National Park Service leased an Aérospatiale SA-315B Lama helicopter from a private operator for search-and-rescue operations primarily in Denali National Park. This allowed the pilots to become intimately familiar with the Alaska Range and develop a close working relationship with the mountaineering rangers. In addition to having the ability to land in tight locations, the Lama can safely land as high as the summit. This high-altitude helicopter has dramatically changed the safety and response time for evacuating sick and injured climbers.

The use of short-haul transfers (transporting rescuers one hundred feet under the helicopter, utilizing a doubled rope) has made insertions of rescuers or extractions of the injured an extremely fast and safe procedure. The Aérospatiale SA-315B Lama has been very effective in using this method. From 1991 through 1998, the Lama rescued sixty-three climbers.

CHAPTER 2
Flying the Iron Road to Fairbanks

*I*n early June 1924, a twenty-five-year-old pilot by the name of Noel Wien arrived in Seward, Alaska, on a steamer from Seattle. He came with a crated J-1 Standard aircraft. At dockside, he met up with Bill Yunker, his good friend and mechanic. Jimmy Rodebaugh, a senior conductor on the Alaska Railroad, had hired the two men to work for a new air service in Fairbanks. He also had ordered another Standard and hired a second pilot, Art Sampson.

In 1924, the Alaska Railroad was the only link between Seward, Anchorage, and Fairbanks. There were no roads between the three towns. Rodebaugh's plan for air service resulted in the first scheduled flights in Alaska. Nobody had ever previously flown between Anchorage and Fairbanks. In 1923, pioneer pilot Ben Eielson was just getting his feet wet, flying a Jenny out of Fairbanks, and he had only 24 hours of flight time. Newcomer Wien had more than 538 hours of barnstorming and aerial circus stunt flying.[1]

When the railroad was completed in 1923, Anchorage's population went from 6,000 to 2,000, as most of the railroad workers headed elsewhere. But the locals were optimistic that eventually mining and tourism would kick in and sustain the town. They also saw the advantages of connecting Anchorage to the rest of Alaska by air travel.

Rodebaugh instructed Yunker and Wien to uncrate the Standard at Anchorage and assemble it. Then Wien was to "joy-hop for a while to make expense money."[2] When the people of Anchorage

Noel Wien (standing on cockpit) with Bill Junker (center) and an unidentified man with the Hisso Standard in Anchorage, Alaska, just before their historic first flight from Anchorage to Fairbanks in 1924. **Museum of Alaska Transportation & Industry**

Downtown Anchorage in spring 1924—the same year Noel Wien introduced the frontier town to aviation and flew the first flight from there to Fairbanks. Anchorage Museum of History & Art

Opposite: Anchorage's original airstrip (lower left), south of downtown in the early 1930s. Noel Wien was the first pilot to use this field. In 1924, he used it for demonstration flights and also for the first flight from Anchorage to Fairbanks. Anchorage Museum of History & Art

Hewitts Photo Shop.   C-2   Anchorage Alaska

259

learned their city would have its first airplane, the locals went wild and residents freely donated their time to build a 300-foot-by-2,000-foot airstrip, paralleling what is today Ninth Street, south of downtown. Wien recalled his first flights from this new airstrip. "One thing I remember so well. The field was covered with about three inches of the finest dust I ever saw. When I took off with the wind from the south, the cloud of dust the Hisso [engine] kicked up was big enough to just about cover the entire city of Anchorage. … My first hop was a test hop on June 4, and in the next month I took more than 170 people on local flights, making seventeen hundred dollars for the Rodebaugh Company."[3]

The relatively new Alaska Railroad linking Anchorage to Denali and Fairbanks was a good iron compass for Noel Wien's first Anchorage to Fairbanks flight in 1924.
National Archives

Opposite: This airstrip at Summit, Alaska, was originally built as an emergency airstrip in World War II. When Noel Wien flew the first flight from Anchorage to Fairbanks, an airstrip much like this was prepared for Wien at Cantwell in case of an en route emergency.
©Bruce McAllister

By early July it was time for Wien to ferry the aircraft to Fairbanks. He checked on weather conditions to the north, by simply looking out his hotel window to see if Denali was visible. On July 6, 1924, at 2:30 a.m., Noel Wien and his trusty mechanic, Bill Yunker, took off from Anchorage on the historic first flight from Anchorage to Fairbanks in their modified Standard. For this flight, Yunker had designed an auxiliary 30-gallon tank to fit under the center section of the Standard's upper wing. On the flight, when the main 35-gallon tank ran low, the pilot simply turned a valve to switch to the reserve fuel.

Wien planned a night departure; he figured that there would be less turbulence at night because of the lower temperatures, and at that time of year, he knew there was plenty of light through the night. Wien used an Alaska Railroad map for navigation. Although the scale of the map left much to be desired, the map showed major curves in the railroad and the various stations along the 356-mile route to Fairbanks. Wien figured his route would be about 300 miles if he "straightened out" the doglegs of the rail route.

As they approached massive Denali, Yunker turned from his seat in the front cockpit and indicated with a hand salute how well their trip was going and how beautiful Denali was. "It had appeared to fill half the sky almost from the flight's beginning. Captain George Vancouver of the British Royal Navy had seen this 'stupendous snow mountain' in 1794 from his ship far south in Cook Inlet."[4]

Soon both Talkeetna and Curry came and went, and Denali was over Wien's left shoulder. As they crossed the Continental Divide, Wien added "coals to the fire" as they climbed to 8,000 feet and approached Cantwell, which had a newly built emergency field if they needed to land. But the Standard was performing beautifully, and they soon were on a smooth ride through Windy Pass. The canyon was narrow and deep, and below they could see the railroad track as it went through three tunnels.

As they came out of the mountain range and saw the Tanana River in the distance, trouble loomed. A cloudbank from the ground up to about 10,000 feet obscured much of the terrain. Wien cautiously picked his way through the murk and followed the Tanana, keeping alternative landing sites in mind. At Nenana, conditions picked up, and Wien felt better.

What they thought was cloud was actually smoke, and Wien started thinking about climbing

Opposite: Weeks Field, Fairbanks, 1934. VFSM Noel Wien, 60-959-37, Archives, University of Alaska, Fairbanks

Bennett-Rodebaugh Co., Inc.

Airplane Service

Fairbanks, Alaska   Chas. L. Thompson, Mgr.

PASSENGER AND EXPRESS RATES--1928

Fairbanks to and from	One Pass.	Two or More Pass., Each	Express Per Lb.
Livengood	$ 50.00	$ 37.50	$ .15
Chena Hot Springs	50.00	40.00	.15
Nenana	50.00	40.00	.15
Palmer Creek	75.00	65.00	.20
Manley Hot Springs	100.00	80.00	.25
Circle Hot Springs	100.00	80.00	.25
Circle City	125.00	100.00	.30
Beaver	125.00	100.00	.30
Kantishna	125.00	100.00	.30
Minchumina	125.00	100.00	.30
American Creek	125.00	100.00	.30
Tanana	125.00	100.00	.30
Rampart	150.00	125.00	.40
Fort, Yukon	150.00	125.00	.40
Bettles	175.00	137.50	.40
Wiseman	200.00	150.00	.40
Ruby	225.00	175.00	.50
Chandalar	225.00	175.00	.50
Eagle	225.00	175.00	.50
Tetlin Lake	250.00	200.00	.50
McGrath	250.00	200.00	.50
Tacotna	265.00	212.50	.50
Ophir	265.00	212.50	.50
Flat	300.00	250.00	.50
Iditarod	300.00	250.00	.50
Skeitmut	350.00	275.00	.75
Nulato	350.00	275.00	.75
Bethel	750.00	500.00	1.00
Nome	750.00	500.00	1.00
Kotzebue	750.00	500.00	1.00

BAGGAGE ALLOWANCE--20 Lbs. PER PASSENGER.
GOLD DUST AND FUR--DOUBLE EXPRESS RATE.

above the mess and turning south toward better conditions. He had trouble tracking the railroad, but still thought about landing on it a few times. On their historic flight to Fairbanks, Wien and Yunker had been airborne for three and a half hours. Ten minutes later, Yunker waved his arms and pointed to an experimental farm, which was part of the new college at Fairbanks. Then suddenly on their right, a huge smokestack loomed through the muck. Soon a racetrack appeared, which they were pretty sure was Weeks Field. Wien "was going to land there even if it wasn't, because a racetrack was home for an old barnstormer."[5]

Upon landing, Yunker had a few choice words for Rodebaugh about the 80 miles of smoke they had just flown through. Why hadn't Rodebaugh warned him of the smoke before he had left Anchorage? The Tanana valley had been covered with smoke for two weeks. Why this information was not passed on to them in Anchorage remains a mystery to this day. The snafu was a bit surprising because even the army had been sending weather reports to Anchorage at the time of their flight.

Left: Bennett-Rodebaugh Company fare schedule, 1928. Museum of Alaska Transportation & Industry

Opposite: Noel Wien (left) and Carl C. Dunbar at Fairbanks, May 23, 1925. This Hisso Standard was the same make and model aircraft that Wien flew on the first Anchorage to Fairbanks flight in June 1924. Noel Wien Collection, VFSM-60-959-18, Archives, University of Alaska, Fairbanks

Noel Wie
photo

CHAPTER 3
The First Flights over Denali

On August 13, 1930, at 10:45 a.m., Alaskan Airways pilot Matt Nieminen and mechanic Cecil Higgins departed Anchorage in a Fairchild 71 aircraft, NC9153, on a historic first: a flight over the summit of Denali with almost 4,000 feet to spare.[1]

On Nieminen's first attempt of this same feat in April 1930 in a Travel Air 4000 aircraft, he could not make it to the top of Denali, an elevation of 20,320 feet. There had been another failed attempt a few days earlier, when they coaxed the Fairchild to the top of Denali, only to find it obscured by clouds.

On that lucky August 13 (a Wednesday, not a Friday), the Fairchild 71 made a relatively quick trip to Denali, 150 miles from Anchorage. The thin air progressively slowed their rate of climb as they passed through 18,000 feet. But the Pratt & Whitney 425-horsepower "Wasp" engine had enough performance to top out at 24,000 feet. Nieminen made circuits around Denali while Higgins took both still photographs and movies. The cabin thermometer read twenty degrees below zero Fahrenheit; if the instrument was

Opposite: On August 13, 1930, in a Fairchild 71 aircraft, Matt Nieminen (opposite) and mechanic Cecil Higgins were the first to fly over the summit of Mount Denali. T. M. Spencer Collection/AHAI

Right: Mechanic Cecil Higgins accompanied Matt Nieminen on the first flight over Denali. Higgins took photographs and movies as they flew over the summit. He was also instrumental in the creation of the Alaska Aviation Heritage Museum in Anchorage. T. M. Spencer Collection/AHAI

accurate, it must have been quite a challenge to keep the cameras working. Somehow, they endured the lack of oxygen for the time they were at high altitude. As mist closed in on the great mountain, the two headed for the "barn"—Anchorage—and safely landed there in the mid-afternoon.

On August 29, 1931, just a bit more than a year after Nieminen's success, Joe Crosson left Fairbanks and flew over the summit in an attempt to accurately measure Denali's elevation. Many Alaskans thought that the mountain might be closer to 25,000 feet than to 20,320.[2] Niemenen's aircraft did not have the sophisticated instrumentation to perform this measurement the year before. On this flight, Crosson's Fairchild 71 was equipped with four altimeters, including a special device from the Weather Bureau that recorded altitude, temperature, and humidity. The press covered the event. Movietone News and Hearst News sent a sound engineer with Crosson and a cameraman on a second Fairchild 71, piloted by Ed Young.[3]

Joe Crosson flying over Denali on August 29, 1931. This was the first flight to establish Denali's elevation; four altimeters on the aircraft corroborated the elevation. A film crew on a second aircraft took the photograph. T. M. Spencer Collection/AHAI

Opposite: Cecil Higgins working on Fairchild 71 aircraft nicknamed Yukon. T. M. Spencer Collection/AHAI

Crosson's Fairchild 71 more than lived up to his expectations, and he noticed that the windward side of the mountain produced updrafts of around 700 feet per minute, aiding his ascent. The film crew took their stills and movies without incident, and the two Fairchild aircraft quickly descended through thickening clouds to refuel at Savage River Camp.

Within six hours of their departure from Fairbanks, they had returned safely, and within weeks the nation was treated to movies of the historic flight. The altimeters showed that Denali, indeed, was very close to 20,000 feet—not 25,000 feet as many had thought.

Joe Crosson took time out from charter flying for this rare candid photograph on July 2, 1933. This photo might have been taken in the Denali National Park area. J. T. Hutchison

Opposite: Joe Crosson (left) at Kantishna airstrip with Ernest Patty, mining engineer, who later became president of the University of Alaska in Fairbanks. Date unknown. Fannie Quigley Collection, 80-46-18, University of Alaska, Fairbanks

CHAPTER 4

Talkeetna: Where the Rivers Meet

*I*ndians lived in the Talkeetna area about 200 years ago, but little is known about their way of life during that time. Few written accounts exist. Fortunately, Shem Pete, a Tanaina Indian who was born about 1896 near Susitna Station, left an oral history of the upper Cook Inlet. Local author Roberta Sheldon noted that the area was inhabited long before the 1800s. "We do know that artifacts located at Stephen Lake, north of Talkeetna, are estimated to be 6,000 years old, indicative of the presence of native people then. Whether these people were Eskimo or Indian, is not known."[1]

In the early 1900s, gold seekers were instrumental in the growth of Talkeetna before the Alaska Railroad made it a key construction camp. Just getting to the Yentna–Cache Creek mining area was a test for the hardiest of individuals. Even the river steamers working their way up the Susitna River to Talkeetna had major problems; ice and logjams could sink them.

From the early 1900s, Talkeetna was closely connected to Denali. In 1910, two climbing expeditions passed through the town, hoping to climb the mountain and also corroborate whether an earlier

Lowell Thomas Jr. took this photograph while on final approach to the old Talkeetna village airstrip in the mid-1960s. Note the Fairview Inn just short of the airstrip (white siding and red roof). Don Sheldon's hangar is just to the left of the airstrip threshold (red building). **Lowell Thomas Jr.**

The Alaska Engineering Commission (AEC) work camp in Talkeetna, 1916. National Archives

Opposite: Talkeetna in 1916. National Archives

MTS. FORAKER AND McKINLEY,
FROM TALKEETNA, ALASKA.

The Japanese "Meji" Denali Expedition poses for a team photograph at Talkeetna in 1960. DENA 17.34

Opposite: A photographer caught this dramatic view of Mount Foraker and Mount Denali from Talkeetna in 1916.
National Archives

expedition by a Dr. Cook had, in fact, made it to the summit of Denali. The logistics of getting to the mountain were formidable. Navigating the unpredictable and dangerous glacier rivers that fanned out from the mountain was a daunting challenge. Early expeditions tried horses, but the animals could not easily make it cross-country; by boat and on foot were the best ways to travel. From those early days, Talkeetna became the staging point for expeditions to Denali and its equally challenging sister peaks. Climbers from all over the world flocked to Talkeetna every year from April through June. In the 1930s, tractors and aircraft helped develop the area. Unlike horses, they did not have to be fed through long winters. Sheldon noted, "The Alaska Department of Natural Resources records describe the first landing strip in the Talkeetna/Cache Creek area:

Early airstrips were usually located on sandbars and were often suitable only for emergency landings. The first field at Cache Creek was located on the divide between Peters and Cache Creeks, near the Talkeetna–Cache Creek wagon road. … in the mid-1930's a new aviation field was built below Thunder Creek, in the Cache Creek valley itself.

That field was 900 feet by 100 feet, and the surface was the gravel bar of the river. … One obstruction on the field was noted: Thunder Creek flows across N. E. end of field."[2]

The rivers surrounding Talkeetna protect the area from excessive development. The town is like an inland island with fifteen miles of spur road separating it from the Parks Highway. The Alaska Railroad has always been the easiest way for tourists to get to the feisty, funky, independent one-street town.

From the 1920s on, roadhouses like the Fairview Inn and the Talkeetna Roadhouse were always welcome sights to pilots, dog mushers, miners, storytellers, and characters of all sorts. Those who passed through usually took rooms and ate home-style meals, which were served at set times. Those who stayed at roadhouses soon got to know each other. Prime Alaska big game specimens adorned the walls and floors, and there were plenty of books for stranded travelers to read.

In the early days of flying, pilots were always especially nice to cooks at the roadhouses, for during winter it was necessary [to drain the oil from air-

For decades, the dining area in the Talkeetna Roadhouse looked much as it does in 2003. Inset, the Talkeetna Roadhouse sign. Photos ©Bruce McAllister

Kitty Banner and Doug Geeting often used the bar at the Fairview Hotel to go over charts and next day's glacier flight schedules. Geeting often plays guitar downtown when off duty. ©1986 P. Parks–Kitty Banner Seemann

Opposite: Fairview Inn, with its old windsock in working order, is close to the final approach to the village airstrip. ©Bruce McAllister

plane engines] into closed containers, [which were] kept in the kitchen overnight. Then, in the morning, the oil had to be heated before being poured back into the engine. … As a result, in the early morning, the roadhouses all had a similar odor—a mixture of warm oil and boiling coffee.[3]

According to an anonymous source, one glacier pilot once almost "took out" the Talkeetna Roadhouse on a "go-around" after an aborted landing one night. Luckily or unluckily, the pilot took out some power lines instead—and survived. Eventually, four large orange balls affixed to the repaired power lines were named in his honor.[4] Such stories may or may not have a grain of truth.

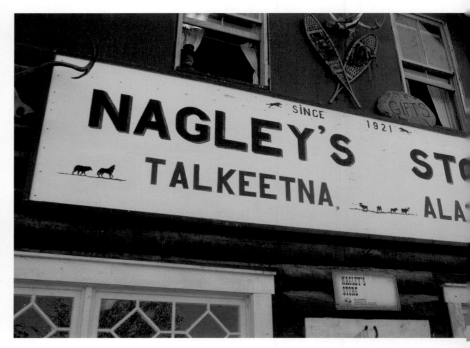

A transportation relic on display in downtown Talkeetna. Right: The store in Talkeetna, which dates back to 1921, originally supplied gold miners. Now it also serves tourists. Photos ©Bruce McAllister

Each of K2 Aviation's two de Havilland DH-C-3T Otters can carry up to 10 passengers plus pilot on flights to Denali National Park. ©Bruce McAllister

Old boots serve as flowerpots in Talkeetna. Climbers from all over the world come here every spring to take on Denali. ©Bruce McAllister

Left: A double rainbow highlights Talkeetna Airport after a rainstorm. Date unknown. ©Dick Stone

Opposite: The annual Talkeetna Flyover is a welcome change from the day-to-day competition between the flying services. Date unknown. Kitty Banner Seemann

CHAPTER 5
Aviation in Denali National Park

The first aircraft to land in Denali National Park was piloted by Colonel Carl Ben Eielson, considered by many to be the father of Alaskan aviation. The event, commemorated by a sign at the spot the wheels touched down, occurred on June 17, 1924. On board the plane was Jack Tobin, a prospector. The landing—and the significance of it—was largely unnoticed.

On April 25, 1932, Joe Crosson, a renowned bush pilot, made the world's first ski-landing on the Muldrow Glacier in Denali National Park. In a Fairchild 71 aircraft, to which he had fitted a pair of

Original sign commemorating the first aircraft landing in Denali National Park on June 17, 1924. Colonel Carl Ben Eielson, considered by many to be the father of Alaska aviation, was killed while on a rescue mission near Siberia just five years after his landing in Denali. DENA 1692

Opposite: Noel Wien used a Fairchild 71 aircraft to drop supplies to a Denali expedition in the early 1930s. Drop zone appears to be McGonagall Pass. DENA 3065

Loading supplies on the Stearman C2B and Fairchild 71 aircraft at Nenana for the Carpé-Koven Expedition in 1932.
Lillian Crosson Collection

Opposite: The Fairbanks Fire Department watered down this field so that Jerry Jones could fly the ski-equipped Stearman from the field to rescue an ill climber on Denali. Lillian Crosson Collection

Above: Jerry Jones (left) and Joe Crosson on Muldrow Glacier with Jones's Stearman C2B. Crosson's Fairchild 71 is in the background. Lillian Crosson Collection

Left: Pilot Jerry Jones helped Joe Crosson supply the Carpé-Koven Expedition on the Muldrow Glacier. Later, Jones rescued one of the climbers (Edward Beckwith), who had fallen ill. Lillian Crosson Collection

Opposite: Joe Crosson departs Muldrow Glacier in a Fairchild 71 (far left of photo) to drop supplies at the Carpé-Koven Expedition upper camp, while Jerry Jones in the Stearman C2B awaits his return. Lillian Crosson Collection

skis, he hauled supplies to Allen Carpé's ill-fated expedition. (Carpé and Theodore Koven would later become the first climbing victims on Denali.) Crosson's departure from Muldrow Glacier was not as successful as his landing. Attempting an uphill takeoff, he did not have enough altitude to clear the surrounding ridges and had to abort the departure. Luckily, he did not damage the aircraft. The climbing party came to his aid on snowshoes, and the next day the winds shifted so that he could take off downhill into the wind.

A week later, Crosson and fellow pilot Jerry Jones returned to Muldrow in two aircraft loaded with supplies: the Fairchild 71 under Crosson's command and a Stearman C2B piloted by Jones. Crosson did not want any heavy landings this time around, and with two aircraft, he could keep the payloads at a more reasonable weight. Tragedy had struck down the Carpé-Koven party in the meantime, and a second climbing party, the Lindley-Liek group, found the campsite abandoned by Carpé-Koven party, complete with diaries and valuable

Members of the Lindley-Liek Expedition pose for a photo before their expedition in 1932. DENA 3065B

photographic film. Soon they discovered Koven's body and eventually came to the conclusion that Carpé had fallen down a crevasse. Thus ended the first aircraft operations on a glacier in Denali. By 2002, ninety-two climbers had perished on the

Super Cub and huskies take a breather at Wonder Lake, 1975. The Cub might have been re-supplying a ranger patrol in Denali National Park. DENA 11.165

Left: A Waco Cabinplane (YKS or YKC Model) re-supplying a survey party in Denali National Park. The Waco was a good performer at high altitudes and was often flown in this area by Haakon Christensen, one of the first pilots to land climbers on Denali. Date unknown. DENA 3064

In 1955, a congressional delegation used an Air Force C-47 to tour Denali National Park. DENA 28.41

The Denali and McKinley airstrips are near the main entrance to the park. Kantishna and Stampede are the only airstrips within the park where aircraft can land—unless there is a qualifying emergency. Helicopters cannot land within the boundaries of the park without prior authorization from the superintendent. And the National Park Service requests that all pilots maintain a minimum distance of 2,000 feet from the nearest groundmass to minimize wildlife disturbance. Search-and-rescue flight refueling operations usually occur outside the boundaries of Denali National Park—either in Talkeetna or through in-flight refueling, employing Hercules aircraft. With these restrictions, the National Park Service has been able to keep aircraft operations within Denali under control—for everyone's benefit.

Above, left: What appears to be a Fairbanks Air Service Super Cub had a rough off-field landing in Denali National Park, 1947. DENA 9.1

Above, right: Laurence Rockefeller and his family arrive in a Beech 18 aircraft at Denali National Park in the 1950s. He was noted for his interest in conservation and protection of wildlife. DENA 28.66

Piasecki H-21 helicopters participated in the mission. The U.S. Army then claimed Moore's feat as a new world altitude record for landing and taking off in any type of aircraft. Unfortunately, the record did not hold up for long. In 1960, a Pilatus Porter landed at almost 17,000 feet in the Himalayas, and shortly thereafter, a Helio Courier landed at 17,500 feet on Mount Logan in the Yukon.

Thus, Terris Moore introduced the Piper Super Cub to Alaska. It has since become the classic Alaska bush plane, and further modifications (such as tundra tires) have made it invaluable in the Arctic.

A Super Cub flying over Denali National Park. Date unknown. ©Dick Stone

CHAPTER 7
Bradford Washburn: Denali's Talented Pioneer

*M*ountaineer, cartographer, aerial photographer, and pilot Bradford Washburn is closely associated with Denali. He has climbed Denali three times, and his wife, Barbara, was the first woman to make the ascent (with him in 1947). By 1999, he had made sixty-six trips to Alaska, breaking new trails on almost every trip. Along the way, he mapped Denali, pioneered new routes up the mountain, tested arctic gear and clothing for U.S. military forces, participated in the first helicopter landings on the Muldrow Glacier, and accomplished numerous other "firsts."

Above: Bradford and Barbara Washburn at their home in Boston, Massachusetts, October 2003. ©Bruce McAllister

Opposite: Windstorm on Denali, 1942. ©Bradford Washburn—Courtesy Panopticon Gallery, Waltham, MA

Over eight decades, he took superb unique aerial photographs of Denali in all of its moods. He always took his photos in what professional photographers call the "sweet light." His windows for doing aerials were the first hour and a half after sunrise and the hour and a half just before sunset. These shooting "windows" afforded him a chance to capture the dramatic shadows and superb three-dimensional views of Denali.

Born June 7, 1910, in Boston, Massachusetts, Washburn took up photography in 1924 when his mother gave him a box Brownie. By 1929, he had graduated to a 4x6-inch Ica Trix camera, which held

According to Bradford Washburn, this is the best shot ever taken of him with his camera equipment. The photograph was taken in 1938 in Cordova, Alaska. Washburn is on the left and pilot Merritt Kirkpatrick is on the right. Camera on left is a Fairchild K-6 and the one on the right is a K-3B, with a DeVry motion picture camera on top. Washburn feels that the oxygen he used on his aerial photography trips (green tanks shown) helped him to take more and better pictures. Aircraft in background is a Bellanca Skyrocket. ©Walter "Knobby" Clark—Bradford Washburn Archives

Bradford Washburn (left) and an unidentified man at Denali National Park. Date unknown. **DENA**

Right: Bradford and Barbara Washburn on the summit of Mount Bertha, Alaska, 1940. She was the first woman to ever climb Denali, and her husband climbed it three times. ©Tom Winship—Courtesy Panopticon Gallery, Waltham, MA

up until his first ascent of Denali in 1942. On vacations in Europe with his family, he spent a great deal of time climbing mountains and developed a keen eye for photographing mountain landscapes.

In 1929, he entered Harvard College. The Depression was not an easy time for anybody, much less a student working his way through college. As the U.S. economy continued to falter, he led climbing expeditions and took to the lecture circuit to keep up his tuition payments. Graduate work at Harvard led him into cartography and expeditions in the Yukon and Alaska. He found a strong sponsor in the National Geographic Society. He also found time to earn his pilot's license in 1934 in a Fleet Model 2 biplane with a 100-horsepower Kinner K5 engine.

Don Sheldon and his Super Cub aircraft at 5,305 feet on Denali in 1955. An early climber, Dr. Frederick A. Cook, falsely claimed that this location was 15,400 feet on Denali's flanks. ©Bradford Washburn—Courtesy Panopticon Gallery, Waltham, MA

Opposite: A team backpacking supplies in support of the 1951 map and geological survey of Denali. Expedition leader Bradford Washburn was also testing his theory that Denali's West Buttress offered a safer, shorter way to the summit than the northeast route. An Air Force C-47 aircraft supported the expedition at lower altitudes, and Terris Moore's Super Cub landed supplies as high as 10,100 feet. National Archives

Denali, as the highest peak in North America, was a magnet for Washburn and his multifaceted talents. Terris Moore (see Chapter 6) flew many missions in support of Washburn's first Denali expeditions, but because Moore was president of the University of Alaska, his schedule could not include supporting Washburn's time-consuming mapping trips. Ultimately, Washburn needed a dependable and available pilot for his Denali projects. He chose Don Sheldon, a young and promising glacier pilot in Talkeetna, who needed long-term contracts. He took an immediate liking to Sheldon, and he later recalled in Sheldon's biography, *Wager with the Wind*, "Don is a rare combination of warmth and efficiency, mirth and seriousness, conservativeness and just sheer guts. Few professional pilots are blessed with his refreshingly youthful joy at drinking in the wonders of the country over which they ply their daily trade—and few pilots anywhere on earth have such a superb spot in which to ply it."[1]

Over the next few decades, Washburn pioneered the West Buttress route to the summit of Denali, and with his camera and cartography, he mapped the mountain for the many climbers who would follow him. Later, Washburn mapped the Grand Canyon and Mount Everest. The Queen of England and the Kingdom of Nepal honored him for his work on Everest.

At 93, during an interview in the Boston area, Bradford Washburn was still as sharp as ever and his boyish enthusiasm for aerial photography had not diminished. He recalled his high-altitude photography flights and asserted that the supplemental oxygen he took on those flights enabled him to shoot more images than he would have without it and also helped him to improve the composition of his dramatic aerial portraits of Denali. Asked about his favorite developer for processing black-and-white film, he shot back, "Kodak D-76, eighteen minutes" (processing time) without hesitation and then went on to show his favorite shots of Denali. Ironically, one of them was not an aerial, but an infrared telephoto shot of Denali from Wonder Lake.[2]

Bradford Washburn has a lifetime of memories of the Great One, Denali, and his aerial photographs of the mountain are a very important part

This 1953 infrared photograph showing Wonder Lake and Denali is one of Bradford Washburn's favorite views of the mountain. ©Bradford Washburn—Courtesy Panopticon Gallery, Waltham, MA

of its history. Just before Ansel Adams died, he made the following observations about his good friend Bradford Washburn:

Brad's aerial photographs of McKinley [Denali], however, are far more [heroic and exciting than climbing to the summit]. It is astounding to realize what tremendous physical risks he took to get these shots—many, for instance, were taken from unpressurized airplanes or helicopters, often at temperatures far below zero, with the door removed and Brad tethered to the opposite side of the cabin. ... Brad's aerial photographs of the McKinley [Denali] landscape are the very first of their kind and still the finest ever made of the great natural landmark.[3]

Lowell Thomas Jr. (left), Barbara and Brad Washburn, and Talkeetna Air Taxi pilot David Lee. Photo taken in the late 1980s. Lowell Thomas, Jr.

Opposite: Sunset at 41,000 feet, Denali, 1978. ©Bradford Washburn—Courtesy Panopticon Gallery, Waltham, MA

CHAPTER 8
The Airplane Doctor

Jim "Hutch" Hutchison of Fairbanks "was perhaps the finest aviation mechanic Alaska has seen."[1] In 1919, he arrived in Alaska as a GI stationed at Fort Liscomb at Valdez. After his release from the army in 1922, he headed for Fairbanks where he landed a low-paying job on the local baseball team. Soon, to make ends meet, he started working at a

Jim "Hutch" Hutchison took this photograph on a swift repair that he and others did on Wiley Post's aircraft after it flipped at Flat, Alaska, in July 1933 while on a round-the-world trip. Post had flown a very long leg from Siberia and was exhausted when he landed, which contributed to this mishap. While his aircraft was being repaired in record time (seven hours), he was put to bed.
J. T. Hutchison

hardware store and doing maintenance work for a local mining company.

In 1925, Ben Eielson and Noel Wien had both started to fly out of Fairbanks, and there was an immediate need for mechanics. "Woodworkers, mechanics, garage men, truck drivers, cat operators … used to hang around the fields in the early days."[2] "Wrong Font" Thompson of the local paper bragged, "There are a hundred volunteers of the Mechanician Class in our town … who can assemble an airship in less than no time."[3] But few could troubleshoot or fix an aircraft like Hutchison.

Hutchison's first break came when Noel Wien asked him to repair a Standard J-1 biplane that had crash-landed on a sandbar on the Toklat River, southwest of Fairbanks. As word of his talent for repairing damaged aircraft spread, Hutchison traveled throughout the Territory of Alaska repairing wrecks. "His specialty was welding," according to his daughter Marion Acord.[4] In the 1920s and 1930s, his services were in great demand. Hutchison once bragged, "There's no plane an Alaska mechanic ever fixed up in the hills that wasn't able to fly back to its home base."[5]

Hutchison once survived for more than a month alone at Kantishna, in Denali National Park, repairing a badly damaged Stinson. He lived in a trapper's

Hutchison (left) with fellow mechanic Larry Yetter. Date unknown. J. T. Hutchison

Opposite: A candid photo of Hutchison in the Interior Airways maintenance hangar in Fairbanks in the 1950s. J. T. Hutchison

*After Wiley Post and his aircraft, the "Winnie May,"
made an unplanned landing and stop at Flat, Alaska, his
good friend Joe Crosson (shown in photo) brought
Hutchison and other mechanics and parts from Fairbanks. They repaired the aircraft in just seven hours.*
Anchorage Museum of History & Art

cabin and "kept the wings in a tent hangar and built
a whole new truss-work with sixty splices in the ribs
and cap-strips."[6] In later years, he fabricated tubular
heaters (which fed off the engine exhaust) for Joe
Crosson. In 1929, Hutchison was called in to do
repairs on the landing gear of Harold Gilliam's aircraft, which was part of the Eielson Relief Expedition near Siberia. That he could weld in extreme
arctic temperatures in high winds was nothing short
of miraculous.

"In January 1930, on a flight in support of the
rescue operation, 'Hutch' was flying with Pat Reid
when their aircraft crash-landed at the headwaters
of the Ungalik River. 'Hutch' patched the plane with
wood from gas boxes and frozen clothing so the
flight could continue."[7] "So there we are," Hutchison
said. "I had my welding gear but no tanks. I did have
three wooden gas cases full of airplane supplies.

This photograph of Wiley Post might have been taken after his forced nap while field repairs were being made on his Lockheed Vega "Winnie Mae" in Flat, Alaska, during his round-the-world flight. Anchorage Museum of History & Art

Opposite: A field repair on a Wien Airlines Fairchild aircraft in late 1920s or early 1930s in interior Alaska. It appears that major engine repairs were a priority. Three felled trees were used to make a quick A-frame to help remove the engine. Frank Henrikson

You're not supposed to use nails in the wing, but we didn't have much choice. I took those boxes apart and very carefully took all the nails out. When we finished that thing, you looked at the wing and saw the words 'Standard Oil, 80 Octane' on the end of the gas case nailed on the spar."[8]

He worked on almost every make and model aircraft that surfaced in Alaska beginning in the 1920s, including exotic and ungainly aircraft like Cunningham Hall, Lockheed Vega, Travel Air 6000, Boeing 247, Stinson Tri-Motor, and DC-2, 3, and 4.

"Hutch [Hutchison] was the dean of the bush mechanics and took care of the bush ships for first one pilot and another all through the bush pilot's era," according to Bud Helmericks.[9] His client list read like the who's who of early Alaska aviation. "Over the years he worked with Ben Eielson, Wiley Post, Noel Wien, and other pioneer pilots. Asked who was the most skillful bush pilot among them, Hutchison replied, 'They were all good. They all survived, so they had to be good.'"[10]

At Hutchinson's ninetieth birthday, Jim Magoffin, president of Interior Airways scratched out a poem to his top mechanic and called attention to his frequently used expression "ippus pippus," meaning "A-okay!"

1900 was the year
That little Hutch did first appear
To live an almost perfect life
With a real productive wife.

He was the bugler every morn
Who'd wake 'em with his noisy horn
And when they marched off to be fed
Hutch would crawl back into bed.

The kids were coming mighty fast
He thought each one would be the last
He had to stop his little games
'cause they were running out of names.

He raised them all though it was tough
To see that each one had enough
Clothes and moose meat by the ton
And guns and rods for everyone.

His trade was fixing things real good
With torch and lathe he always could
Make 'em stronger than when new
And usually run much better, too.

And though he's turned 90 now
He still can show the young guys how
To fish and shoot; oh, what a guy!
His formula is old Ten High.

So here's to Hutch, our lifelong friend
We will love him 'til the end,
And as long as he is with us
Everything is ippus pippus!!![11]

Hutchison tinkering with a Model T Ford before a Fairbanks parade. Date unknown. J. T. Hutchison

One of Hutch's fellow aircraft mechanics in Fairbanks in the 1930s was "Tillie" Tilman who was the flight mechanic for pilot Ed Young. In that era, Young was one of the best pilots to work for. According to Tilman:

He liked the way I maintained and repaired aircraft and I liked to fly with him, for he was careful and took everything into consideration. He was a very safe pilot. I repaired a lot of airplanes in those years, but I never had to fix one that Ed Young broke. … I flew with him mainly in Fairchild 71s. … the skis used on those planes for winter flying weighed 165 pounds each. They were 11.5 feet long and 18 inches wide. Fairbanks carpenter Charley Schiek steamed and bent hardwood to

Ed Young with a Fairchild 71 aircraft nicknamed 'Denali,' circa 1930. Tillie Tilman considered Young to be one of the very best pioneer pilots because he took good care of each aircraft he flew. Young's career ended prematurely when his aircraft crashed at Livengood, north of Fairbanks. George Ed Young Collection, Folder 43, Accession 81-24-184, Archives, University of Alaska, Fairbanks

make them. The Fairchild Co. made pedestals for them, but they weren't much good until Fairbanks aircraft mechanic Jim "Hutch" Hutchison welded on more tubes to beef them up. They had a big steel shoe for a tail skid, and Hutch welded some Stellite on the bottom for better steering.[12]

Hutchison installed a temporary heating system in Joe Crosson's Curtiss Super Swallow aircraft. The double tube system took heat from the exhaust and kept the crew members' feet warm during long flights. J. T. Hutchison

Tillie Tilman recalled the early days of aviation in Fairbanks.

Weeks Field, in Fairbanks, was a short runway in those days, and in winter we were always afraid of going through the Northern Commercial Co.'s cordwood pile at the east end. Many times Ed [Young] had to chop the power on takeoff when he could see we weren't going to make it. As that big radial engine started to roar and we would start down the runway I would be thinking, 'Will we, or won't we …'

When we aborted, sometimes we'd drain a little fuel, or leave a little freight, but seldom did Ed offload the flight mechanic.

All the mechanics—Hutchison, [Gordon] Spring-bett, [Orval] Porter, Jack Warren, and company official Hjalmar Nordale—were at the airplane when we'd leave for our weekly trip, and all of them would shake our hands before we'd climb into the Fairchild.[13]

Mechanics designed this Pacific Alaska Airways display for the annual North America Sled Dog Championship parade in Fairbanks around 1937, featuring a Lockheed 10 aircraft. J. T. Hutchison

Opposite: Noel Wien's Hisso Standard aircraft needed a helping hand after it bogged down on the airstrip in Circle Hot Springs in 1925. Circle Hot Springs was the first government-approved airstrip in the Alaska territory. **Anchorage Museum of History & Art**

For almost sixty years, Hutchison worked as an aviation mechanic for and with Alaska's great pioneer pilots. His numerous awards from the state of Alaska and the FAA were rewards not only for his aircraft modifications but also for his can-do attitude. When Hutchison signed off on aircraft repair, the pilot could take off without any worries.

Harold Maness, an aviation mechanic in Talkeetna in the 1960s, worked on Don Sheldon's aircraft. He recalled that Sheldon was always watching the bottom line on maintenance costs.
Kitty Banner Seemann

CHAPTER 9
The Glacier Pilots

The town of Talkeetna, tucked away in Alaska's Susitna Valley, is the staging area for climbers hitching rides to the 7,200-foot Kahiltna Glacier. Thus, it has always been home to Denali's glacier pilots, who have often fought tooth and nail for the business of tourists and the nearly one thousand climbers who attempt to reach the summit of Denali every year.

Don Sheldon had by far the highest profile of all the glacier pilots. Sadly, his colorful career ended when he lost his battle with cancer in 1975. During his twenty-seven years of flying out of Talkeetna, he averaged 800 flight hours a year and never seriously injured himself or any of his passengers.

In 1938, Sheldon and a buddy (with but $12 between them) took the Alaska Railroad from Anchorage to Talkeetna. They found lodging in a homesteader's cabin. One morning before sunset, Sheldon heard a noise at the front door. He confronted a huge bull moose that he promptly dispatched with a .250 Savage rifle. Within hours, Sheldon traded two quarters of moose for a couple of bags of sugar and flour. Thus Sheldon began his life in Alaska. He later spent some time at the University of Alaska in Fairbanks. Eventually, he had a hankering to take up flying when he saw how important it was in Alaska. After working for contractors who were building airstrips all over Alaska,

Don Sheldon participating in the rescue of some Denali climbers in May 1960.
©Grey Villet/Time Life Pictures/Getty Images

Sheldon moved to Anchorage where he took lessons at the Lars Larson Flight School at Merrill Field. After six hours of instruction, he was doing solo flights and enjoying his time in a variety of aircraft—the J-3 Cub, the J-5 Cub, and the Aeronca. As World War II approached, Sheldon joined a crew which was building the McGrath airstrip. When the airstrip was near completion, he joined the Civilian Pilot Training Corps, which he hoped would get him into the army as a pilot.

But that was not to be. He ended up as a gunner on bombers flying from England to the heartland of Germany; he made twenty-six combat missions in all, earning the Distinguished Flying Cross and other air medals. When Sheldon returned to the United States, he began ferrying new aircraft for Piper. Soon he wondered how and when he could purchase one for himself. During the war, he had saved all his of pay for the day he might acquire two aircraft. But there was a demand for Pipers, and the waiting list was too long for the eager Sheldon.

Finally, on the return leg of a ferry flight to Mexico, Sheldon found his first aircraft, a military surplus L-2M Taylorcraft. Although the fabric covering had partly dried out, there were only 60 hours on the tachometer. The harsh southwest sun had taken its toll. But by 1950, he had restored this small, but versatile aircraft and landed some profitable government contracts to fly out of Talkeetna.

The first year was make-or-break for Sheldon. He had several rough experiences. On a flight to pick up some moose quarters near a small lake in the Talkeetna Mountains, his float-equipped Taylorcraft stalled on a very tight takeoff run—fifty feet off the water! That he and his passenger were not killed was a miracle. Sheldon was able to hike out to get help for his passenger. He then nicknamed the lake Eight G Lake.

That same year he ran out of fuel one night on a government charter and miraculously dead-sticked his aircraft on the tundra next to a large beaver pond. As if these two experiences were not traumatic enough, in the fall of the same year he ran into severe turbulence on a flight to Anchorage and almost lost the left wing of his newly acquired PA-14 Super Cub. Utilizing his previous aerobatic training, Sheldon survived this controlled crash thanks to some forgiving cottonwoods that cushioned his landing. The PA-14 was a total loss, and he eventually sold it for $50 minus the engine.

His company, Talkeetna Air Service, had lost two planes, but he and his partner, "Stub" Morrison, realized that they would have to hustle some new, more lucrative contracts. At this point, Sheldon hit pay dirt in the person of Bradford Washburn, an explorer, climber, and photographer who had embarked on a "long-term study of Denali and its neighboring peaks, a study that would culminate in the first detailed large-scale map of the mountain and would require 15 long years of arduous work to complete."[1] Washburn had worked on Denali with other gifted pilots, including Dr. Terris Moore, president of the University of Alaska; but he needed a pilot who could stay on until the end of the project. He knew that Sheldon was the man, and his good friend Bob Reeve told him, "I've heard a lot about that kid [Sheldon], and he's either crazy and is going to kill himself, or he'll turn out to be one hell of a good pilot!"[2] Over the next several years, Sheldon and Washburn worked as a team on Denali. On one occasion, Washburn instructed Sheldon—over the

Don Sheldon taking a break on Denali between flights. Date unknown. **Museum of Alaska Transportation & Industry, Wasilla**

phone from Boston—where to land on the high peaks of Denali to rescue a woman climber. His instructions were perfect. And many times, Sheldon rescued sick climbers and transported the bodies of those who had died off the mountain. Looking back over his career, Sheldon recalled, "I've owned a lot of planes, 45 at last count, and I've demolished a few, but I've never lost a single passenger."[3]

Another former Talkeetna operator, Lowell Thomas Jr., made more than a dozen rescues on the high peaks of Denali in about 3,000 hours of mountain and glacier flying. A former World War II Air Force flight instructor and former lieutenant governor of Alaska, Thomas is typical of the pilots who understand and appreciate the demands of flying in Alaska. He recalled two dangerous moments. In the first, he pulled off a dead-stick landing of his wheel/ski–equipped Helio Courier on the banks of the Susitna River; and in the second, he suddenly lost four inches off one of his propeller blades on a flight to Anchorage. Thomas commented, "I am convinced that the good Lord has been my copilot many times. … I have experienced only five mechanical failures; all have ended happily with nary a crash."[4]

Two famous Alaska bush pilots, Sig Wien and Harmon "Bud" Helmericks, often reviewed accident reports in Alaska and concluded that once a problem was found it could be solved—but the difference between pilots who survived and those who didn't was simple. "It [the accident] just didn't happen to us." Andy Anderson, a fellow Arctic pilot, once told Helmericks, "So many things happen every day that we don't even know how close we could have come to having an accident."[5]

Over the years, Talkeetna's feisty glacier pilots developed some glacial relationships and rivalries, sometimes stealing customers from each other. There is only so much pie to go around because the climbing season is only three or four months long each year, and the winters with no business are long.

Don Sheldon and two brothers, Glenn and Cliff Hudson, had one of the more "robust" rivalries. "Things got so bad that Sheldon's Cessna allegedly once buzzed Cliff Hudson's PA-20 at close range [reported to be 25 feet], an incident that led to an

---

Don Sheldon with three of his Piper Cubs in the early 1950s. Museum of Alaska Transportation & Industry, Wasilla

Lowell Thomas Jr. with his Helio Courier, Anchorage, September 2003. ©Bruce McAllister

Opposite: Holly Sheldon, Don Sheldon's oldest daughter, took up flying, and in the fall of 2003 she earned her commercial pilot's license. ©Bruce McAllister

Vern Tejas after first successful solo winter ascent of Denali in 1988. He had an easy ride down the mountain in Lowell Thomas Jr's Helio Courier. Lowell Thomas Jr.

Opposite: Cliff Hudson and his Super Cub getting ready to depart a riverbed in the Denali region in the 1970s.
©Jim Sharp

investigation by the Federal Aviation Administration."[6] In another supposed encounter, Cliff Hudson's aircraft prop blew snow into Sheldon's hangar, which prompted Don Sheldon to chase Hudson's aircraft with a ball-peen hammer, as Hudson tried to make a quick getaway.[7] Finally, the FAA in Anchorage held a hearing; the report included some of the pilots' statements: "It was a struggle to make a living. Ill will developed. It was a race to get business. We stole each other's passengers a number of times."[8] An encounter was described: "During January … Hudson parked an automobile in front of an aircraft Respondent was taxiing along a road in Talkeetna. On Hudson's refusal to move the car a fight ensued in the village store resulting in physical injuries to Respondent and Hudson and damage to store property. Hudson said, 'He hit me in the jaw and I poked him in the nose a couple of times.'" And the record noted: "Respondent's animosity was heartily reciprocated by Hudson."[9]

Frances "Twigg" Twigg, the oldest pilot (and still reputedly the best dancer) in Talkeetna in 2003, started flying for Don Sheldon in the 1950s. He and Don Sheldon pioneered glacier landings on Denali for the climbers. He recalled that they usually carried extra landing gear, props, nuts, and bolts in case they had any misfortunes while landing on the glaciers. They also supplied miners and people who lived out in the bush. Sheldon liked to "bomb" goods to them when he could not land. "Dropping items like pills, medicine, and other things that would fit in the hollow of a roll of toilet paper got to be a game as Don would try to bounce the roll at the feet of the recipient. In case he overflew the target, the unwinding roll of toilet paper would mark the spot."[10]

One Thanksgiving, with Don Sheldon piloting the Super Cub and Twigg as co-pilot/loadmaster, they were supposed to drop a turkey over a lady's cabin near Chilitna Pass. Twigg was a bit too accurate and the eighteen-pound turkey scored a bull's eye right through the roof of the lady's cabin. Luckily, the turkey did not wipe out the recipient! Don turned to his co-pilot and yelled, "Holy Christ, Pedro!" (The good buddies had nicknames: Sheldon was big Pedro and Twigg was little Pedro.)

To this day, Twigg, every bit the survivalist, wears a compass on his shirt. In case all else fails, in the air or in the mall, Twigg will find his bearings. He has a special way of landing on glaciers. After overflying a landing spot on the glaciers going up the mountain, he does a 180-degree turn and flies down the mountain very close to the elevation of his intended landing spot, and at that point he zeros his altimeter. Then, when he sets up for his final approach, he knows approximately what his touchdown point should be for flare-out to landing.

For Talkeetna's choice clientele, no fewer than four operators were vying for business in 1984. And there were probably no more than a dozen qualified glacier pilots flying the various aircraft these outfits operate—everything from a Cessna 185 to a Super Cub, a Helio Courier, a Cessna Propjet 207, and a de Havilland Beaver.

Kitty Banner Seemann was the first woman glacier pilot to "break the ice" in Talkeetna. In 1980,

Top right: Cliff Hudson with Queenie, the dog that survived a 1,000-thousand-foot free-fall into a snow-bank from a Super Cub in the 1950s. The frisky dog accidentally exited the aircraft. Hudson Air Service

Bottom, right: Jay Hudson, Cliff's son, has followed in his father's footsteps and is one of the prime charter operators out of Talkeetna. ©Bruce McAllister

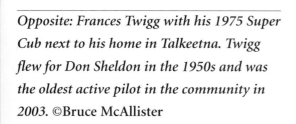

Opposite: Frances Twigg with his 1975 Super Cub next to his home in Talkeetna. Twigg flew for Don Sheldon in the 1950s and was the oldest active pilot in the community in 2003. ©Bruce McAllister

Right: Kitty Banner fueling a Cessna aircraft before hauling climbers to Denali. Date unknown. ©Roger Robinson

Seemann and her partner, Kimball Forrest, started K2 Aviation, after she earned her spurs working for another operator in Talkeetna for a couple of seasons. Seemann worked hard preparing herself to fly the glaciers. Early in her flying career, she had pumped fuel at Boulder airport in Colorado, taken aircraft mechanic's courses in the Denver area, and been an expediter for an energy company in Alaska. She also had flown cross-country with a stunt pilot in an old Luftwaffe trainer, a Bucker-Jüngmann biplane, and

dreamed of the art of flying—not just the mechanics of it. She then found a great instructor, a woman by the name of Carolyn Cullen, at an all-women's airfield on Martha's Vineyard. Cullen was a charter member of the "Ninety-niners," an exclusive organization of women pilots started by Amelia Earhart. Cullen wanted to teach Seemann to be competitive in male-dominated commercial aviation. "Cullen had the blunt mannerisms of a roughneck; Banner [Seemann] had the total inability to look anything but feminine, whether she was wrestling fuel drums . . . or loading a pickup."[11] Cullen taught Seemann well, and soon K2 Aviation was holding its own in the business of hauling climbers to Denali. Seemann was intimidating to some of the more chauvinistic climbers—but only because she was so professional. Like Don Sheldon, Kitty Seemann attracted media attention during her career as a glacier pilot.

Kitty Banner displays her catch while on a successful fishing trip to a high-altitude lake near Talkeetna. Date unknown. Kitty Banner Seemann

Opposite: Kitty Banner with a K2 Aviation Cessna 185 near Ruth Gorge. Date unknown. Kitty Banner Seemann

Jim Okonek, owner of K2 Aviation in the late 1980s, recently recalled, "Each of us considers himself the best pilot in town, and it's hard for us to imagine why a person would ever want to fly with anybody else."[12]

Although some of the original companies are still in business, the rivalries at this time are less noticeable. There is plenty of business for all the operators. On a typical day, one might see tourists from Japan filling an oversized Turbine Otter and park rangers loading up a Cessna 185 to carry them and their raft to a remote location within Denali National Preserve.

The pilots from various operators now get along. They all make timely position reports as they fly up to, around, and over Denali. Glacier pilots use checkpoints as they report their position to other pilots when they fly in the Denali area. The

Jim Okonek operated K2 Aviation for several years. Before that he was a helicopter pilot, and in 1979 and 1980, he flew Hughes 500 Series and Bell 206 helicopters as high as 14,000 to 16,000 feet, rescuing mountain climbers. ©Bruce McAllister

more common checkpoints are Archdeacon's Tower, Mount Deception, Gun Sight Pass, 747 Pass, Base Camp, Great Gorge, Moose's Tooth, North Summit, One-Shot Pass, Peters Dome, Sourdough Gully, South Summit, and Wickersham Wall. According to legend, 747 Pass earned its name for a foreign carrier that flew through it en route to Anchorage. The carrier was not known for its navigational skills.

The following poem captures some of the challenges confronting glacier pilots—past, present and future.

Doug Geeting with one of his Cessna 185 aircraft, September 2003. In one of his notorious flights, he rescued climbers in whiteout conditions after navigating between peaks in zero visibility. ©Bruce McAllister

The Bush Pilot
Bob Johnson, 1942[13]

Typical airman of Alaska …
    Serving men
With wings o'er snow-covered
    Tundra and ice-filled streams—
Mud-clogged roads—following
    'Cat' tracks to miners' shack.
Or sourdough's fire, siwashing
    Cold and alone,
No storm too bad, weather too
    Cold for mercy flight.
No field too small or load
    Too large—
Ingenious man bridging any gap
    Of necessity to bring—

Men–Mail–Meat to lonely outposts—
    Returning with gold or fur.
One-man airline–owner–operator–
    Crew chief–traffic,
Competent pilot far afield from
    Carrier's deck,
Courageous and willing servant
    Of Alaska's people—
Too few we have filling the gap 'tween
    Dog sled and transport
Making Hero's flight as daily duty—
    Unacclaimed.

In July 1993, this K2 Aviation aircraft made a forced landing on unfriendly terrain near Denali. There were no injuries. Lowell Thomas Jr.

CHAPTER 10
The Denali Guardian Angels

Looking out from inside Frances Randall's tent at the Kahiltna base camp, June 1982.
Lowell Thomas Jr.

Base camp managers on Denali are the last link climbers have with the world before they set out to ascend the mountain. They are also master expediters, radio operators, weather forecasters, and social workers. They keep everyone in camp upbeat.

Frances Randall, who served as manager of the Kahiltna Glacier Base Camp (altitude 7,000 feet) from 1976 until 1983, set the standard for base camp managers. For climbers, pilots, and anyone else connected to Denali, Randall was truly the angel of Denali. Cancer claimed her life in 1984, but this extraordinary woman's talents will never be forgotten. Mount Frances in Denali National Park was named in her honor after her death.

Frances Randall taking a break at the Kahiltna base camp, July 1982. Lowell Thomas Jr.

Opposite: Frances Randall playing the violin at the Kahiltna base camp, June 1982. Lowell Thomas Jr.

Lowell Thomas Jr. (left), Frances Randall, and Walter Cronkite at the Kahiltna base camp, Denali, June 1982. Cronkite was taking a break from a CBS film project on Ruth Glacier. Lowell Thomas Jr.

Opposite: Tents of a German climbing group at Kahiltna base camp, May 1982. Lowell Thomas Jr.

Randall's love affair with Denali started in 1964, when she, her husband (whom she later divorced), and a seasoned group of climbers from a group called the Seattle Mountaineers set out to climb Denali. After taking a train from Anchorage, they traversed miles of tundra, crossed two rivers, and systematically worked their way up the mountain. On July 9, all but three of the group made it to the top from their last camp, which was at 17,800 feet. At the time, this group was the largest to make a successful ascent of Denali; the effort was also noteworthy because the group was the first to communicate with the outside world by a battery-operated transmitter as it made the final climb.[1]

Over the next few years, Frances Randall became one of the legends of Denali. Glacier pilot Cliff Hudson of Talkeetna hired her to manage the base camp on Kahiltna Glacier, and she made a lasting impression on all the climbers who took on the challenge of climbing Denali. When she was not managing the base camp during the summer climbing season on Denali, she was teaching violin to children in Fairbanks and was playing violin in the Fairbanks Chamber Orchestra. When she was not at home in her log cabin in Fairbanks or running the base

camp, she found time to climb five of the six highest mountains in North America.[2]

From 1991 to 2000, "Base Camp Annie" Duquette ran the camp at Kahiltna, continuing the great tradition of Frances Randall. An amusing story she recalled from her years on the mountain was that of "a Japanese 'climber' [who] got off the aircraft with two Samsonite suitcases and a shopping bag. His first question was 'Where is the Mount McKinley [Denali] walking path?'"[3]

Don Sheldon's mountain house on Ruth Glacier, Denali, May 1982. The house serves as an overnight destination for climbers when it gets busy at base camp. Inset: The base camp medical tent at 14,200 feet on Denali, September 1983. Lowell Thomas Jr.

Right: Annie Duquette at the Kahiltna base camp in the 1990s. Annie Duquette

Kahiltna base camp landing site, at the southeast fork of the Kahiltna Glacier. Ski tracks show between the shadows. Elevation at this strip is 7,200 feet. Lowell Thomas Jr.

There were some harrowing events during Duquette's tenure on the Kahiltna Glacier. A climber had fallen into a dangerous crevasse and into water at the bottom of it. An Aérospatiale Lama helicopter had to short-haul him out because he had become so heavy from falling into the water in the crevasse. Duquette herself had a sobering experience. She had been on at base camp for five years and was doing the standard probing for crevasses around the area. Upon setting up her tent and staking down a supplies sled, she suddenly lost her probe down a bottomless crevasse. She was standing just outside the entrance to her tent! From that time on, Annie was very careful about not taking anything for granted in what she now remembers as the crevasse minefield on Denali.

These two base camp managers ran a tight ship on Denali. They probably saved lives with their resourceful communications and kept climbers happy when things were not going smoothly on the mountain. Their diplomatic skills came in handy when they had to interrupt flight schedules and when they served as a communications link between search-and-rescue aircraft and climbers.

A K2 charter aircraft "hung up" a ski as it landed on the Kahiltna Glacier in June 1980. When base camp manager Frances Randall first viewed this incident, she called out on the radio, "Would the K2 aircraft please right itself?" On the slopes of Denali, Randall kept everybody loose. Kitty Banner Seemann

CHAPTER 11
Search and Rescue

One of the first search-and-rescue operations in the Denali area occurred in 1938 when the engine of Frank Barr's American A&E Pilgrim Model 100-B aircraft blew a cylinder on a supply flight between Big Delta and Chicken, Alaska. With a payload of nearly 2,000 pounds of diesel, the Pilgrim lost altitude quickly, and Barr wisely set it down on a 4,000-foot ridge. Although he had picked the best place to land, moss had hidden jagged rocks that tore up the rear end of the fuselage as he touched down. His aircraft's heavy payload contributed to a relatively hard landing.

But Frank Barr was a seasoned bush pilot who knew about survival and the country he was flying. "When trouble came, the bush pilot had to be a cook, hunter, trapper and woodsman rolled into one if he was to survive an unscheduled stop in the wilderness. There were twenty-two forced landings reported to the authorities in Alaska in 1937. Nearly all of the pilots survived. ... the pilots had on-the-job training at picking out landing sites in an instant."[1]

Opposite: A Bell 212 helicopter, piloted by Ron Smith, makes a rescue on the South Buttress of Denali at 12,000 feet in 1984. ©Roger Robinson

Above: Frank Barr in 1936 at Juneau with his favorite aircraft, an American "Pilgrim" 100-B.
Delano Photo—Courtesy of Jim Ruotsala

Frank Dorbandt's damaged Ford Tri-Motor aircraft is hoisted to a good repair site at Flat, Alaska. Search and rescue was not necessary in this case; mining equipment came in handy. Date unknown. **Museum of Alaska Transportation & Industry**

Maps in 1938 were close to worthless, but Barr knew the country like the back of his hand. In addition, at that time, two-way radios were not yet in wide use, and he had only an unworkable receiver used for monitoring code transmissions. But Barr, a veteran who had hundreds of hours of bush-flying experience in the Yukon and southeastern Alaska, had emergency equipment that included a couple of rifles, mosquito netting, an axe, dried food, rice, fishing gear, cooking gear, matches, some airplane dope, and tape.

In those days, with a small aircraft population, Alaskans kept tabs on flights and when one went missing, word spread quickly. Fairbanks Mayor Les Nerland quickly mobilized the citizenry to support and finance a quick search-and-rescue effort. The *Fairbanks Daily News–Miner* noted: "Lack of governmental provisions for such searches, which come periodically, is to be regretted and in time may be

On Mount Deception, near Denali, in November 1944, a U.S. Air Force C-47 aircraft dropped supplies and rations for recovery of a military C-47 aircraft that crashed on the mountain. Crampons are strapped to man's back (foreground). Robert Reeve Collection, 93-183-70, University of Alaska, Fairbanks

U.S. Army Sergeant Francis Dowdy and dog, Paratrooper Joe, of the 10th Rescue Unit from Ladd Air Force Base, Fairbanks, rehearse a jump from a Douglas C-47 aircraft. Date unknown. National Archives

obviated. … today an emergency exists that calls for spontaneous action."[2]

Many pilots and airlines joined in the intensive search for Barr which lasted more than a week. The Pollack Flying Service Bellanca took 144 aerial photographs of hundreds of square miles of wilderness along Barr's route of flight. After six aircraft had come close to Barr's position and missed seeing his signals, Barr changed his signal strategy for the next search aircraft: He used tape to make a sign that read GRUB on his aircraft's wings, and he made another sign that read JOSEPH VILLAGE on the top of the fuselage. (Joseph Village was where he intended to hike out to.) As soon as he heard another aircraft near his position, Barr quickly lit some diesel fuel to make a good smoke signal.

His luck changed, and pilot Jim Dodson spotted Barr's signal pyrotechnics. Within hours, a Wien Alaska aircraft dropped a map and survival gear to enable Barr to hike to a pickup location. After nine days in the bush, Barr was home in Fairbanks and in one piece. Nobody was surprised because everybody knew about Barr's knack for surviving tough situations.

Later, Barr insisted on recovering and fixing up his wounded Pilgrim. "When I flew an airplane for a while, it was my friend. I wouldn't think of leaving one out in a swamp somewhere. I always picked them up and brought them back."[3]

Today, the Denali National Park Service coordinates search-and-rescue efforts for Denali. The staff includes mountaineering rangers who are assisted by volunteer rangers out of Talkeetna from April through mid-July. To cover interior Alaska and Denali National Park during nonclimbing months, Alaska Air National Guard officers and enlisted men run the Rescue Coordination Center twenty-four hours a day from a single room at Fort Richardson near Anchorage, Alaska. The officers and enlisted men, like their counterparts at Denali National Park, coordinate which resource will go to the incident site; they also supply coordinates and other critical information. The rescue could include civilian charter aircraft or military helicopters accompanied by Lockheed Hercules that can refuel other helicopters in the air. When the military participates in the rescue operations, it usually sends along Alaska Air National Guard Para-rescue personnel, known as PJs. (In World War II, they were known as para-jumpers—hence the abbreviation PJs.) The rescue force could also include a civilian helicopter or even

A Piasecki H-21 Workhorse helicopter tests skis at Summit Lake near Denali at 10,000 feet in 1960. Airglas Engineering Company

Opposite: This restored Piasecki H-21 Workhorse helicopter played an important role in search-and-rescue operations on Denali in the 1960s. ©Bruce McAllister

A Japanese climber with badly frozen feet is carried to a Helio Courier aircraft for evacuation from Denali. Date unknown. Lowell Thomas Jr.

Opposite: Major Scott Coniglio on duty at the Alaska Air National Guard's 11th Rescue Coordination Center at Fort Richardson, Alaska. The center coordinates search-and-rescue operations in Alaska's vast interior and supports the Denali National Park Talkeetna Ranger Station search-and-rescue operations during Denali's climbing season. ©Bruce McAllister

snowmobiles. Emergency Locator Transmitters (ELTs) are mandatory on cross-country aircraft in Alaska, and many sportsmen take them along when they go into remote areas. There are typically more than five hundred ELT activations a year, but only about 10 percent are real incidents. On jet airliners in Alaskan airspace, ELTs that have been stored in passengers' baggage have frequently gone off, prompting erratic and moving targets for the satellites that download the information to the Rescue Coordination Center. New 406 ELTs communicate with a new generation of satellites and can provide the owner's type aircraft, home telephone number, and even the exact coordinates of the ELT's position.

Normally each spring, the U.S. Army's 4th/123rd Helicopter Company (based at Fort Wainright, in Fairbanks, Alaska) sets up the HART (High-Altitude Rescue Team) Base Camp at the 7,200 feet on the Kahiltna Glacier below Denali; the helicopter company also supports a high-altitude camp at

---

An Alaska Air Guard Boeing CH-47 Chinook prepares to land at 14,000 feet during a major Denali rescue operation in 1998. ©1998 Scott Darsney

Left: An Alaska Air National Guard Boeing CH-47 Chinook unloads supplies at 14,000 feet on Denali. Date unknown.
©Roger Robinson

Right: An Alaska Air National Guard Boeing Chinook CH-47 makes a hoist on Denali. Date and location unknown.
©Roger Robinson

14,200 feet. Nicknamed the "Sugar Bears," the unit uses specially equipped Chinooks that have modified engines.

Some of the rescues have been spectacular, but the pilots involved always give fair credit to the PJs, who swing out of the helicopters and somehow haul in climbers who could have everything from extreme frostbite to serious heart problems or pulmonary edema. Colonel Ron Parkhouse, who in May 1991 landed an H-60 "Pavehawk" helicopter at 14,400 feet on Denali to rescue a South Korean climber, recalls that his two PJs had the "toughest job on the rescue mission and did a phenomenal job."[4] He remembers that at the time his helicopter had no power margin and could only hover at two feet above the rescue site. Colonel Parkhouse and his

Left: Alaska Air Guard Boeing CH-47 Chinook on Kahiltna Glacier during the major Denali rescue operation in 1998. ©1998 Scott Darsney

Opposite: Interior of an Alaska Air National Guard Boeing CH-47 Chinook during the major Denali rescue operation in 1998. ©1998 Scott Darsney

During a search-and-rescue operation, an Aérospatiale SA 315B helicopter descends from 14,000 feet on Denali. Date unknown.
©Roger Robinson

Opposite: Rigging a short haul line at 14,000 feet to a Aérospatiale Lama SA 315B helicopter during a major Denali rescue operation in 1998. ©1998 Scott Darsney

crew received Airmen's Medals for their roles in that mission.

Backcountry common sense could save the need for many search-and-rescue operations. Some rescues have strikingly similar scenarios: climbers not knowing their own limitations, pushing the weather, pushing the clock (being caught by darkness while still en route), and so on. Denali expert Bradford Washburn listed several things climbers could do to improve their chances of survival on Denali: "Unless your party is uniformly powerful and experienced, employ a guide who is both. … Don't climb too fast, even if the weather or the nearness of the summit tempts you to hurry. If you are ill at high altitude, go down three or four thousand feet. … if you are caught on the trail in one of McKinley's [Denali's] fiendish blizzards, don't push on, no matter how near the summit may be. Go back to camp or settle down in a well-equipped bivouac. Have a good sleep and try it again when the weather clears."[5]

Opposite: This Alaska Air National Guard flight crew landed a Sikorsky MH-60 "Pavehawk" helicopter at 14,400 feet on the slopes of Denali in May 1991. Pictured: Pilot-Major Ron Parkhouse (second from left), Co-pilot Lt. Colonel Terry Graybeal (second from right), Flight Engineer Master Sergeant John Fild (far right). Man on left and one in center unidentified. Michael R. Echola—Alaska Air National Guard

CHAPTER 12
Denali from Above

Denali is a photographic paradise. The moods of the mountain are endless, and so are the photographic possibilities for those with a camera and plenty of film. The great aerial photographer Bradford Washburn (see Chapter 7) sees the mountain in a unique way—in dramatic, almost three-dimensional black-and-white photographs that are truly fine art. Many of the exceptional photographs of Denali share one thing in common: They were taken in the sweet light—the first hour or two or the last hour or two of daylight.

Many of the photographs in this chapter were taken by pilots and climbers who have worked on Denali entire seasons and in all kinds of weather. In some cases, they were participating in search-and-rescue operations. Photographers (as well as tourists) may wait weeks for a momentary "window" to see and photograph the "Great One." Luckily, on the one day in September 2003 that the author (as a passenger on a charter flight) flew around the mountain, the weather was perfect.

Flying down the Ruth Gorge near Denali. ©Bruce McAllister

An avalanche on Mount Foraker. Lowell Thomas Jr.

Opposite: Mount Hunter. ©Bruce McAllister

Camp at 14,200 feet on Denali. Lowell Thomas Jr.

Climbers on Denali Pass. Lowell Thomas Jr.

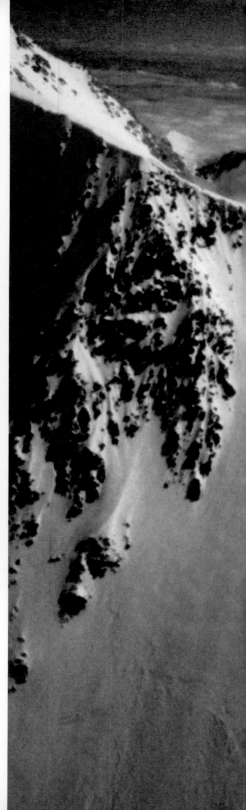

Left: Glacial pools in the Don Sheldon amphitheater on Denali.
©Amy B. Whitledge

Right: Inside "Star Wars" in the Great Gorge on Denali. ©Amy B. Whitledge

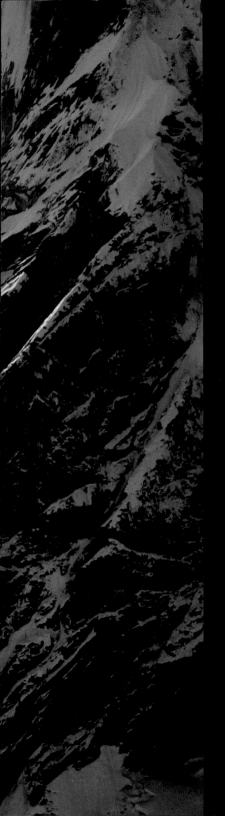

Left: Flying through the Great Gorge. ©Bruce McAllister

A view of the Great Gorge on Denali. Mount Dickey is on the left. ©Amy B. Whitledge

Left: Three rivers, the Chulitna, Susitna, and Talkeetna, meet at Talkeetna. ©Bruce McAllister

Right: Denali's two summits. The South Summit (the higher of the two and on the left) reaches a height of 20,320 feet. ©Amy B. Whitledge

Notes

Introduction

1. John McPhee, *Coming into the Country,* p. 174.
2. Bradford Washburn and David Roberts, *Mount McKinley—The Conquest of Denali,* p. 23.
3. Ibid.
4. Bradford Washburn, *A Tourist Guide to Mount McKinley,* pp. 15–16.
5. Constance Helmericks, *We Live in Alaska,* p. 260.

Chapter 2

1. Ira Harkey, *Pioneer Bush Pilot—The Story of Noel Wien,* p. 73.
2. Ibid., p. 74.
3. Ibid., p. 75.
4. Ibid., p. 79.
5. Ibid., pp. 82–83.

Chapter 3

1. Robert W. Stevens, *Alaskan Aviation History,* Vol. 2, p. 907.
2. Dirk Tordoff, *Mercy Pilot—The Joe Crosson Story,* p. 155.
3. Ibid., p. 156.

Chapter 4

1. Roberta Sheldon, *The Heritage of Talkeetna,* pp. 1–2.
2. Ibid., p. 87.
3. Rudy Billberg, *In the Shadow of Eagles,* p. 104.
4. Anonymous source.

Chapter 5

1. Bradford Washburn and David Roberts, *Mount McKinley—The Conquest of Denali,* pp. 103–104.

Chapter 6

1. Letter from Terris Moore to Dr. William Wood, President Emeritus, University of Alaska, June 23, 1982.
2. Ibid.
3. Ibid.

Chapter 7

1. James Greiner, *Wager with the Wind—The Don Sheldon Story,* p. 7.
2. Bradford Washburn interview by Bruce McAllister, October 13, 2003.
3. Bradford Washburn and David Roberts, *Mount McKinley—The Conquest of Denali,* p. 17.

Chapter 8

1. Jim Magoffin, *Triumph over Turbulence,* p. 54.
2. Jean Potter, *The Flying North,* p. 120.
3. Ibid., p. 120.
4. Marion Acord telephone interview by Bruce McAllister, June 1, 2003.
5. Jean Potter, *The Flying North,* p. 120.
6. Ibid., p. 121.
7. Jim Magoffin, *Triumph over Turbulence,* p. 54.
8. Gerry Bruder, *Heroes of the Horizon,* p. 165.
9. Harmon Helmericks, *The Last of the Bush Pilots,* p. 216.
10. *Fairbanks Daily News-Miner,* February 11, 1988, p. 5.
11. Jim Magoffin, *Triumph over Turbulence,* pp. 59–60.
12. *Fairbanks News-Miner,* Heartland Section, May 21, 1989, p. H-9.
13. Ibid., p. H-10.

Chapter 9

1. James Greiner, *Wager with the Wind,* p. 71.
2. Ibid., p. 79.
3. Ibid., p. 141.
4. Fred Hirschmann, *Bush Pilots of Alaska,* p. 8.
5. Bruce McAllister, *Wings Above the Arctic,* pp. 103–104.
6. *Smithsonian,* January 1989, "Daredevil Pilots Take Glacier Flying to New Heights," p. 104.
7. Ed Cole interview by Bruce McAllister, July 25, 2003.
8. Roberta Sheldon, *The Heritage of Talkeetna,* pp. 148–149.
9. Ibid., p. 149.
10. Joe Rychetnik, *Alaska's Sky Follies,* p. 44.
11. *Alaskafest,* June 1981, "The Wings of Her Dreams," p. 26.
12. *Smithsonian,* January 1989, "Daredevil Pilots Take Glacier Flying to New Heights," p. 105.
13. Alaska Centennial Commission, *Honoring 100 Alaska Bush Pilots,* 1967, p. 24.

Chapter 10

1. Frances Randall, *Denali Diary—Letters from Denali,* p. xv.
2. Ibid., p. xvii.
3. Annie Duquette interview by Bruce McAllister, October 22, 2003.

Chapter 11

1. Dermot Cole, *Frank Barr—Bush Pilot in Alaska and the Yukon,* p. 65.
2. Ibid., p. 65.
3. Ibid., p. 70.
4. Colonel Ron Parkhouse, USAF, telephone interview by Bruce McAllister, September 16, 2003.
5. Bradford Washburn and David Roberts, *Mount McKinley—The Conquest of Denali,* p. 149.

Bibliography

BOOKS

Billberg, Rudy (as told to Jim Rearden), *In the Shadow of Eagles.* Alaska Northwest Books, Portland, Oregon, 1992

Bowers, Don (creator and original author), *The Alaska Airmen's Association Logbook* (Third Edition; Spring 2001). Alaska Airmen's Association, 4451 Aircraft Drive, Anchorage, Alaska 99502

Bruder, Gerry, *Heroes of the Horizon.* Alaska Northwest Books, Portland, Oregon, 1991

Carey, Mary, *Alaska—Not for a Woman.* Branden Press, c/o Mary's Fiddlehead Fern Farm, Talkeetna, Alaska, 1975

Colby, Merle, *A Guide to Alaska.* MacMillan, New York, 1943

Cole, Dermot, *Frank Barr—Bush Pilot in Alaska and the Yukon.* Alaska Northwest Books, Portland, Oregon, 1986

Coombs, Colby, *Denali's West Buttress.* Mountaineers Books, Seattle, 1997

DeCaneas, Antony (editor), *Bradford Washburn Mountain Photography.* Mountaineers Books, Seattle, 1999

Drury, Bob, *The Rescue Season.* Simon & Schuster, New York, 2001

Garrett, Ron, *Life at the Talkeetna Roadhouse.* Alien Publishing, Spokane, Washington, 1998

Gilbert, James, *The Great Planes.* Grosset & Dunlap, New York, 1970

Greiner, James, *Wager with the Wind—The Don Sheldon Story.* Rand McNally & Company, New York, 1974

Harkey, Ira, *Pioneer Bush Pilot— The Story of Noel Wien.* University of Washington Press, Seattle, 1974

Helmericks, Constance, *We Live in Alaska.* Garden City Publishing, Garden City, N.Y., 1944

Helmericks, Harmon. *The Last of the Bush Pilots.* Alfred A. Knopf, New York, 1977

Hirschmann, Fred, *Bush Pilots of Alaska.* Graphic Arts Center Publishing, Portland, Oregon, 1989

Hommer, Ed, and Daniel Paisner, *The Hill.* Rodale Press, Emmaus, Pennsylvania, 2001

Juptner, Joseph P., *U.S. Civil Aircraft Series,* Volumes 1-6. Aero Publishers, Los Angeles, 1962

McAllister, Bruce, *Wings Above the Arctic.* Roundup Press, Boulder, Colorado, 2002

McIntyre, Rick, *Denali National Park—An Island in Time.* Sequoia Communications, Santa Barbara, California, 1986

McPhee, John, *Coming into the Country.* Farrar, Straus, and Giroux, New York, 1976

Magoffin, Jim, *Triumph over Turbulence.* Jim Magoffin, Fairbanks, 1993

Mergler, Wayne (editor), *Last New Land—Stories of Alaska Past & Present.* Alaska Northwest Books, Portland, Oregon, 1996

Mills, Stephen, *Arctic War Planes—Alaska Aviation of WWII.* Bonanza Books, New York, 1978

Mills, Stephen, and James Phillips, *Sourdough Sky—Bush-Flying Interior Alaska.* Bonanza Books, New York, 1960

Mitchell, Ruth, *My Brother Bill.* Harcourt, Brace & Company, New York, 1953

Molina, Bruce/Alaska Geographic Society (Volume 9, Number 1), *Alaska's Glaciers.* Alaska Geographic Society, Anchorage, 1982

Moore, Terris, *Mt. McKinley, The Pioneer Climbs.* University of Alaska Press, Fairbanks, 1967

Potter, Jean, *The Flying North.* MacMillan Company, New York, 1955

Randall, Frances, *Denali Diary—Letters from McKinley.* Cloudcap Press, Seattle, 1987

Rychetnik, Joe, *Alaska's Sky Follies.* Epicenter Press, Seattle, 1995

Sheldon, Roberta, *The Heritage of Talkeetna.* Talkeetna Editions, P.O. Box 292, Talkeetna, Alaska 99676, 1995

Sherwonit, Bill, *Denali—A Literary Anthology.* Mountaineers Books, Seattle, 2000

Sherwonit, Bill (editor), *Alaska Ascents.* Alaska Northwest Books, Graphic Arts Imprint, Portland, Oregon, 1996

Stevens, Robert W., *Alaskan Aviation History,* Volumes 1 and 2. Polynyas Press, Des Moines, Washington, 1990

Time-Life Books (Epic of Flight Series), *The Bush Pilots.* Time-Life Books, Alexandria, Virginia, 1983

Tordoff, Dirk, *Mercy Pilot—The Joe Crosson Story.* Epicenter Press, Kenmore, Washington, 2002

Ulibarri, George (compiler), *Guide to Federal Archives Relating to Alaska.* University of Alaska Press, Fairbanks, 1983

Washburn, Bradford, *A Tourist Guide to Mount McKinley.* Alaska Northwest Publishing, Anchorage, 1971

Washburn, Bradford, and David Roberts, *Mount McKinley—The Conquest of Denali.* Abradale Press–Harry N. Abrams, New York, 1991

Waterman, Jonathan, *In the Shadow of Denali.* Dell Publishing Group, New York, 1994

MAGAZINES & ARTICLES

Anchorage Centennial Commission, *Honoring 100 Alaska Bush Pilots*, June 1967,p. 22

AlaskaFest (Alaska Airlines Complimentary Magazine), June 1981, "The Wings of Her Dreams," pp. 24–27

Alaska Geographic, Volume 25, Number 4, 1998, Frontier Flight (Special Issue)

Alaska History, Volume 9, Number 2, Fall 1994, "Airplanes on Denali," pp.1–12

National Geographic, August 1953, "Mount McKinley Conquered by New Route," pp. 219–248

National Geographic, August 1992, "Denali, Alaska's Wild Heart," pp. 63–87

Smithsonian, January 1989, "Daredevil Pilots Take Glacier Flying to New Heights," pp. 96–107

About the Author

A longtime resident of the Colorado Rockies, Bruce McAllister is a freelance photographer, writer, and pilot who has logged many of his 4,800 hours of flight time in the Alaska Arctic, the Northwest Territories, the Yukon, and the Alaska Highway. His previous three books, *Wings Across America* (with Jesse Davidson), *Wings Above the Arctic*, and *Wings Over the Alaska Highway* (with Peter Corley-Smith), have received acclaim for their photography and unusual stories.

The aircraft in the background is a beautifully restored 1928 J5 Travel Air Model 4000, with a 9-cylinder Wright "Whirlwind" engine, courtesy of Dan Murray, Longmont, Colorado. ©Brian Patarich